BASEBALL
THE · AMERICAN · EPIC

SHADOW BALL

THE HISTORY OF THE NEGRO LEAGUES

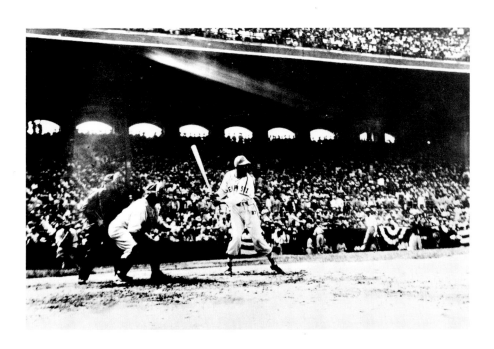

BY GEOFFREY C. WARD
AND KEN BURNS, WITH JIM O'CONNOR

ILLUSTRATED WITH PHOTOGRAPHS

ALFRED A. KNOPF ❦ NEW YORK

Photo credits:
Archive Photos: 71; Associated Press: 63, 74, 76; Bettmann Archive: 62;
Brooklyn Public Library: 54, 61 *(top)*; Chicago Historical Society: 17; Phil
Dixon: 27 *(top)*; Mary R. Eckler: 44; William Gladstone: 52; Dennis Goldstein:
24 *(center right)*, 25, 34, 45; Hal Lebowitz: 38; Los Angeles Dodgers,
Inc./Maurice Terrell: 49; Jerry Malloy and Negro Leagues Baseball Museum,
Inc.: 7; National Baseball Library & Archive, Cooperstown, New York: title
page, 5, 8, 10 *(bottom)*, 12, 13, 14, 15, 18, 19, 21, 22, 24 *(center left, bottom)*,
26–27 *(bottom)*, 28, 29, 30, 31, 32 *(left)*, 33, 35, 36, 37, 39, 40-41, 47, 48, 51,
53, 56, 58, 61 *(bottom)*, 68, 69, 70, 72, 73, 75, 78–79; Buck O'Neil: 32 *(right)*;
Ohio Wesleyan University: 43; Joseph M. Overfield: 9; The Sporting News: 16
(bottom), 23, 57, 65; Sports Illustrated/Mark Kauffman: 42; Sports
Illustrated/Neil Leifer: 67; John Thorn: 59; Transcendental Graphics/Mark
Rucker: 4, 10 *(top)*, 11, 20; UPI/Bettmann: 55, 60; Western Reserve Historical
Society: 16 *(top)*, 46.

THIS IS A BORZOI BOOK PUBLISHED BY ALFRED A. KNOPF, INC.

Library of Congress Cataloging-in-Publication Data
Burns, Ken.
Shadow Ball : a history of the Negro leagues / Ken Burns,
Geoffrey C. Ward, with Jim O'Connor.
p. cm. — (Baseball, the American epic)
Includes index.
ISBN: 0-679-86749-X (trade) — ISBN: 0-679-96749-4 (lib. bdg.)
1. Negro leagues—History—Juvenile literature. 2. Baseball—United
States—History—Juvenile literature. [1. Negro leagues—History.
2. Baseball—History.] I. Ward, Geoffrey C. II. O'Connor, Jim. III. Title.
IV. Series.
GV863.A1B87 1994
796.357'0973—dc20
94-5552

Manufactured in the United States of America
2 4 6 8 0 9 7 5 3 1

CONTENTS

CHAPTER 1

A GENTLEMAN'S AGREEMENT.

The crowd stirs with anticipation as the Indianapolis Clowns, an all-black team, take the field for their warm-ups. The second baseman's glove snaps back when he snags a quick peg from first. He hurls the ball to the third baseman, whose diving catch brings the fans to their feet. Then a batter steps to the plate. The pitcher sets, gets his signal, winds up, and throws. The batter swings. He hits it! The shortstop leaps to his right and makes a tremendous backhand stab.

He jumps up, whirls, and throws to first just ahead of the sprinting runner. The low throw kicks dirt up by the first baseman's outstretched glove. The runner is out! The crowd roars.

But wait! There's no ball in the first baseman's glove. The batter didn't really hit it. The Clowns were warming up in pantomime—hurling an imaginary ball so fast, making plays so convincingly, that fans could not believe it wasn't real.

They called it shadow ball—and it came to stand not only for the way the black teams warmed up, but the way they were forced to play in the shadows of the all-white majors. Many black ballplayers were as good—if not better—than the big leaguers. All that kept them out was the color of their skin.

Since the mid-1800s, baseball has been played by young and old, rich and poor, men and women, in big cities and tiny villages across the country. It is the all-American game.

But for years baseball team owners and managers, players and even fans, did everything they could to keep African Americans from playing on professional teams. To some whites, the idea of being struck out by a black pitcher or throwing a home run pitch to a black batter was unthinkable.

In 1867, just two years after the end of the Civil War, which freed African Americans from slavery and promised them equal opportunities, organized baseball made its first attempts to ban blacks. The National Association of Base Ball Players—which later became the National League—refused to allow an all-black team from Philadelphia to join the league.

Nevertheless, during the next twenty-five years, more than fifty blacks managed to play on white teams. The first was Bud Fowler, born near Cooperstown, New York, in 1858. Fowler was a true all-around player—he was a good catcher, first baseman, and pitcher but was best at second. In 1872 he joined a white professional club in New Castle, Pennsylvania.

Bud Fowler is credited with inventing the first shin guards. White players were spiking him so often that he began taping pieces of wood to his legs to protect himself. And although he batted over .300 every season, no team would keep him very long. As soon as a competent white player came along, Fowler lost his job.

One season he played for five different teams. By the end of his career, Fowler had played for fourteen teams in nine different leagues. Eventually, worn down by years of bouncing from team to team, Fowler returned to Cooperstown and became a barber.

"MY SKIN IS AGAINST ME."

—BUD FOWLER

The first black to make it to the majors was Moses Fleetwood Walker, on Ohio clergyman's son. Walker joined the Toledo Blue Stockings of the American Association as a catcher in 1884 and immediately ran into a wall of racism.

As the catcher, it was Walker's job to tell the pitcher, using hand signals, what kind of pitch to throw next. But one Blue Stockings pitcher ignored Walker's signals because he refused to take orders from a black man.

That pitcher was not alone. There was opposition to black players everywhere. The Buffalo Bisons of the International League, a minor league, signed Frank Grant to play second base. Grant was an outstanding athlete, but like Bud Fowler before him, he was the constant target of white opponents' spikes.

One player, Ned Williamson, vividly recalled Grant's harassment: "The players of the opposing team made it a point to spike this brunette Buffalo. They would tarry at second when they might easily make third just to toy with the sensitive shins of the second baseman. The poor man played only two games out of five, the rest of the time he was on crutches."

Meanwhile, the Newark Little Giants signed fastballer George Washington Stovey, who became one of the dominant pitchers of the International League.

Stovey soon caught the eye of John Montgomery Ward, captain of the New York Giants. In 1887 word got out that Ward wanted Stovey to pitch for the Giants. Cap Anson, manager of the Chicago White Stockings, announced that neither he nor any of his players would ever play a team on which blacks were welcome.

Anson's threat worked. The Giants did not sign Stovey.

"YOU CANNOT HIT 'EM WITH A CELLAR DOOR."

—A REPORTER DESCRIBING GEORGE WASHINGTON STOVEY'S PITCHES

Other baseball officials were just as vocal with their racism. One International League umpire declared that he would always call the close plays against a team that included black players.

The message was clear. That year the owners of all the major league ball clubs entered into a "gentleman's agreement"—an unwritten policy to sign no more black players. The minors formally declared that blacks were no longer welcome.

The color line was being drawn all over the country, and by 1899 blacks were completely out of organized baseball. But they would soon demonstrate—to the delight of fans everywhere—that nothing could keep them from playing the game they loved.

THE CHICAGO WHITE STOCKINGS OF 1888. CAP ANSON *(STANDING, SECOND FROM RIGHT)* THREATENED NOT TO LET THEM PLAY AGAINST ANY TEAM THAT HAD A BLACK PLAYER.

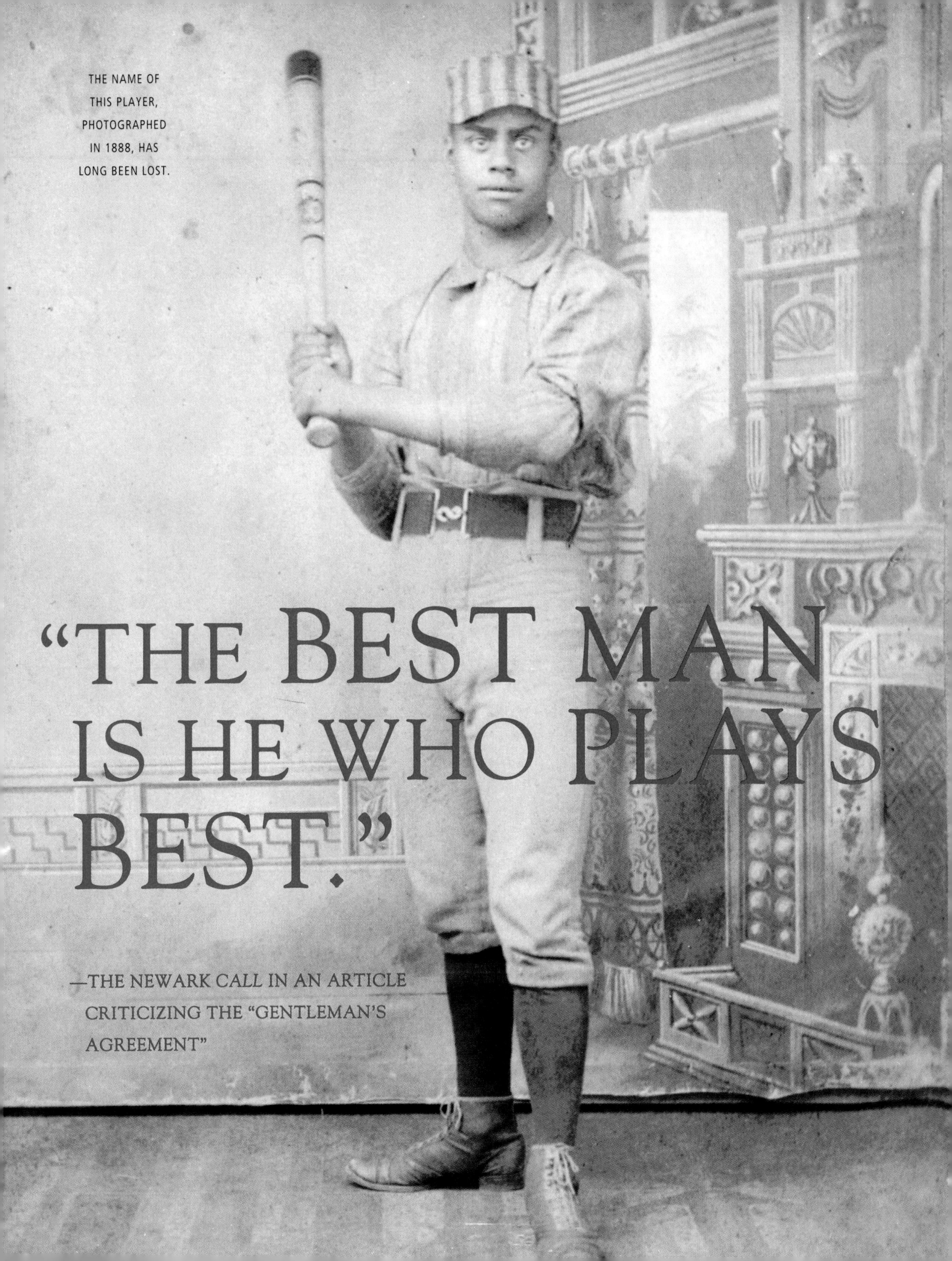

THE NAME OF THIS PLAYER, PHOTOGRAPHED IN 1888, HAS LONG BEEN LOST.

"THE BEST MAN IS HE WHO PLAYS BEST."

—THE NEWARK *CALL* IN AN ARTICLE CRITICIZING THE "GENTLEMAN'S AGREEMENT"

CHAPTER 2

BARNSTORMING. By 1900 America was baseball mad, and the sport had grown into a full-fledged industry. But because of the gentleman's agreement, African Americans—roughly one-tenth of the nation's citizens—were denied jobs in that industry. Black athletes realized that if they were ever going to play professional ball, they would have to form their own teams.

The first professional black team was the Cuban Giants, originally a group of waiters from the Argyle Hotel in Babylon,

Cuban Giants.

COLORED CHAMPIONS.

1887. AND. 1888.

THE CUBAN GIANTS,
ORIGINALLY A GROUP OF
WAITERS FROM NEW YORK

OPPOSITE:
THE CUBAN X GIANTS

Long Island. They called themselves "Cuban" to hide the fact that they were African Americans, and "Giants" (like several other black teams) after the popular all-white New York Giants. It was said that they spoke gibberish to each other in the field so that fans would think they were Spanish.

Soon black fans had dozens of teams to cheer for: the Cuban X Giants, New York's Lincoln Giants, Meridian Southern Giants, Indianapolis ABCs, French Lick Plutos, and the Page Fence Giants.

The all-black teams of the early 1900s spent much of their time on the road. No black team could draw the same crowds as the white professional teams, so in order to make enough money to cover expenses, black teams had to be willing to play all the time.

THE PAGE FENCE GIANTS WERE SPONSORED BY A WIRE MANUFACTURER. WHEN THEY ARRIVED IN A NEW TOWN, THEY WOULD RACE THROUGH THE STREETS ON BICYCLES TO DRUM UP INTEREST IN THEIR GAMES.

"ORGANIZE YOUR TEAM."

— ADVICE TO YOUNG BLACK MEN FROM W. E. B. DuBOIS, CO-FOUNDER OF THE NATIONAL ASSOCIATION FOR THE ADVANCEMENT OF COLORED PEOPLE

They crisscrossed America in buses, traveling wherever there was a team—black or white—that would play them. When the white major league clubs went on the road, black teams rented their stadiums and scheduled doubleheaders. During the winter months they often headed south to Mexico or Cuba and played teams of white all-stars from the major leagues.

Almost every game was an away game, and the road trips stretched for weeks and sometimes months. The players called their nomadic life barnstorming.

It was a tough and wearying way to live. A team might play two or three games in a single day—sometimes in two or three different towns. Then the players would drive most of the night to get to the next day's first game.

It wasn't easy for the teams to find hotel rooms or restaurants—especially in the South, where many states had passed laws legalizing segregation, or the separation of the races. Blacks and whites went to separate schools, ate in separate restaurants, drank from separate water fountains. Black ball teams often had to stay in hotels or boarding houses in the black section of town, or split up and sleep in people's homes. If the weather was warm, they slept on the ground next to the ball field.

Barnstorming brought some of the best players to small towns everywhere. In the days before radio and television, these games were often the only games many fans—black and white—ever saw. Factories and schools closed early when a black team came to town. No one wanted to miss the game.

Two players dominated black baseball in its early years. John Henry "Pop" Lloyd was called "the black Honus Wagner" because he was considered equal to the great Pirate shortstop. Wagner said he was honored to be compared to Pop Lloyd.

SHORTSTOP POP LLOYD PLAYED BASEBALL UNTIL HE WAS 58.

"You could put Wagner and Lloyd in a bag together," said Connie Mack, owner of the all-white Philadelphia Athletics, "and whichever one you pulled out, you wouldn't go wrong."

In the winter of 1911 Lloyd took part in a classic confrontation with another baseball superstar. The other player was Ty Cobb, the white Detroit Tiger center fielder and American League batting champ. Lloyd was playing in Cuba for the Havana Reds, one of Cuba's top teams, when the Tigers came through on a tour.

Cobb, who had hit .385 the previous season, hit a sizzling .370 in Havana. But Lloyd was better—in twenty-two trips to the plate he got eleven hits, for an even .500.

Cobb was also a superb base stealer and bragged that he would show the Cubans how they stole bases in the American League. But Lloyd and Havana catcher Bruce Petway stopped Cobb every time he tried to steal second. When the five-game exhibition series ended, Cobb vowed never to play against blacks again.

The other black star of the era was Andrew "Rube" Foster. Foster had signed with the semi-professional Fort Worth Yellow Jackets when

he was only 17 years old. The massively built young Texan moved up quickly to the Leland Giants and then on to the Cuban X Giants, who were based in Philadelphia. In 1902 the Cubans played an exhibition game against the Philadelphia Athletics. Foster pitched and beat the great Rube Waddell. His teammates nicknamed him Rube in honor of his victory.

The next year John McGraw of the New York Giants came calling. McGraw had been one of the toughest and dirtiest players of his time. He was just as tough as a manager and was always looking for a player who could help his team win. McGraw didn't care what color the player was. In 1901 he had tried to sneak the Page Fence Giants' Charlie Grant onto the Baltimore Orioles by claiming that Grant was a Cherokee named Chief Tokahoma. But Grant had been recognized and never got to play.

"WASTE A LITTLE
TIME ON HIM."

—RUBE FOSTER'S ADVICE TO PITCHERS
FACING A BATTER WHO SEEMS EAGER TO HIT

After that experience, McGraw knew there was no chance of slipping Foster into the big leagues. Instead, he paid Rube to teach Christy Mathewson, the Giants' star pitcher, his "fadeaway," or screwball pitch.

Foster later took most of the Cuban X Giants back to the Leland Giants. In those days it was common for players to jump from team to team, depending on how much money each owner offered. And although the owners believed that players should honor their contracts, there was little they could do when a player left.

Foster was an unbeatable pitcher. In 1904 he won fifty-one games and lost only five, using a combination of physical skill and psychology to dominate opposing batters.

"The real test comes when you are pitching with men on base," Foster said. "Do not worry. Try to appear jolly and unconcerned. Where the batter appears anxious to hit, waste a little time on him. Waste a few balls and try his nerves; the majority of times you will win out by drawing him into hitting a wide one."

In 1911 Foster and John Schorling, a white tavern owner, founded the all-black Chicago American Giants. In addition to being a player and part owner, Rube was also the team's manager. He was about to begin a career that would change black baseball forever.

TWO INNINGS AHEAD OF EVERYONE ELSE. In 1919 the bloodiest race riots since the Civil War swept the United States. The worst took place in Chicago. It started when a black boy was stoned to death because his rubber raft floated too close to a white beach. By the time it ended, thirty-eight people were dead and over five hundred injured. For many of the blacks who had moved north to escape the harsh anti-black laws of the South, the riots confirmed their worst fears—racism was everywhere.

AN UNIDENTIFIED
KANSAS CITY
MONARCHS PLAYER

OPPOSITE THE ST. PAUL
GOPHERS, 1909

PHOT. BY
T.E. MILLER
KC

But as a result of the riots, African Americans began to assert themselves. Marcus Garvey, the black nationalist, urged blacks to look to themselves for help. "No more fears," he wrote. "No more begging and pleading." Blacks began to set up their own businesses. Few would become more successful than Rube Foster.

In the year of the riot, Foster began organizing the Negro National League. He believed that a black-owned and -operated league would keep black baseball from being controlled by whites and would give black players the opportunity to make as much money as white players. And, he said, he wanted to "do something concrete for the loyalty of the race."

There were eight teams in the league: the Kansas City Monarchs, Indianapolis ABCs, Dayton Marcos, Chicago Giants, Detroit Stars,

RUBE FOSTER
(IN JACKET AND TIE)
WITH HIS CHICAGO
AMERICAN GIANTS, 1919

"WE ARE THE SHIP, ALL ELSE THE SEA."

— RUBE FOSTER ON THE NEGRO NATIONAL LEAGUE

St. Louis Giants, Cuban Giants, and Foster's own Chicago American Giants.

The owner of the Kansas City Monarchs was a white man named J. L. Wilkinson. Foster believed that all the clubs should be owned by blacks, but he agreed to let the Monarchs into the league because of Wilkinson's long, impressive history in black baseball. He had founded the barnstorming All Nations team, whose members were black, Indian, Asian, and Hispanic.

Under Rube Foster's leadership, the American Giants seldom lost a game. One year he led them to a 123–6 record. The Giants were so successful that they sometimes drew bigger crowds than the Cubs or the White Sox, Chicago's two white major league clubs.

Foster, one fellow Negro leaguer recalled years later, was always "two innings ahead of everyone else." As a manager, he insisted that his teams play "smart baseball"—a fast, aggressive game built around bunts, steals, hit-and-runs, and crafty pitching.

By comparison, white baseball was a slower, quieter game. After Yankee slugger Babe Ruth belted fifty-four home runs in 1920 and brought thousands of new fans to his team, major league managers built their strategy around hitting the long ball.

No player stayed on Foster's American Giants unless he could bunt a ball into a circle drawn along one of the foul lines. Any Giant who was tagged out standing up had to pay a five-dollar fine. "You're supposed to slide," Foster told them.

The result was a fast-paced, exciting game, and the Negro National League was a huge success. In the 1923 season alone, over 400,000 fans attended league games. Foster's creation became one of the largest black-owned businesses in the country.

YANKEE SLUGGER BABE
RUTH WITH BLACK FANS

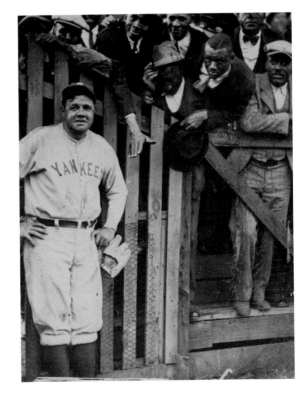

BULLET JOE ROGAN
(BELOW LEFT) OF THE
KANSAS CITY MONARCHS.
HIS "PALM BALL" BAFFLED
EVERY BATTER.

OSCAR CHARLESTON
(BELOW RIGHT), "THE
BLACK TY COBB"

Three players dominated the league: Pitcher Smokey Joe Williams, who stood 6' 5", threw so hard that his team had to change catchers after four or five innings because their hands would swell up from the pounding.

Bullet Joe Rogan could throw heat like Smokey Joe, but he had another weapon in his arsenal. He invented the "palm ball"—a change-up that "walked up" to hitters who were waiting for his fastball. It totally baffled them.

Oscar Charleston was a fierce, hard-hitting center fielder who could outrun any ball. When a young base-ball writer once suggested that Charleston was "the black Ty Cobb," an old-time reporter corrected him. "Cobb," the reporter said, "is a white Oscar Charleston."

The Negro National League's success attracted the attention of a group of white businessmen who saw the profits to be made in black baseball. In 1922 they formed the Eastern Colored League, which included the Philadelphia Hilldales, Brooklyn Royal Giants, Lincoln Giants, Baltimore Black Sox, Atlantic City Bacharachs, and New York Cuban All-Stars.

THE BALTIMORE BLACK SOX

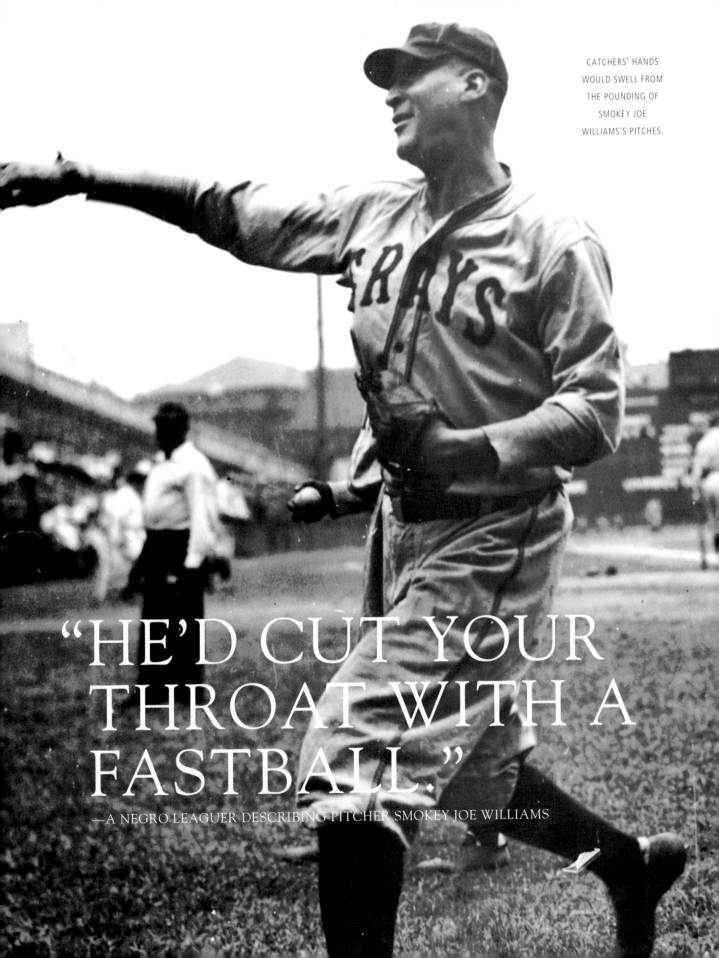

CATCHERS' HANDS
WOULD SWELL FROM
THE POUNDING OF
SMOKEY JOE
WILLIAMS'S PITCHES.

"HE'D CUT YOUR
THROAT WITH A
FASTBALL."
—A NEGRO LEAGUER DESCRIBING PITCHER SMOKEY JOE WILLIAMS

The Eastern League immediately began raiding the Negro National League for its best players. This enraged Foster, and he refused to schedule a World Series that had been planned with the Eastern champion for 1923.

"FOLKS COMING OUT LIKE BEES HIDDEN AWAY ALL WINTER."

—THE CHICAGO *DEFENDER* DESCRIBING OPENING
DAY OF THE 1923 NEGRO LEAGUE SEASON

In 1924 Foster's business sense prevailed, and the first Negro World Series was held between the Kansas City Monarchs and the Philadelphia Hilldales. The Monarchs won in a tough ten-game series.

The emotional and financial strain of running the league—and watching his best players being lured away to the rival Eastern League—started to wear Foster down. In 1926 he suffered a nervous breakdown. One day he was found chasing imaginary fly balls in the street near his house. Finally he was sent to a mental hospital, where he died in 1930.

On the day Foster was buried, one reporter wrote that his coffin was closed "at the usual hour a ball game ends." Three thousand fans braved a cold, icy rain to attend the funeral of the man they called "the father of black baseball."

AT FOSTER'S GRAVESITE, MOURNERS LEFT FLORAL TRIBUTES IN THE SHAPE OF A BASEBALL AND A BASEBALL DIAMOND.

CHAPTER 4

THE GUY PEOPLE WANTED TO SEE. In 1929 the stock market crashed and the American economy collapsed. It was the beginning of the Great Depression. Wealthy people were wiped out overnight, and thousands of homeless families roamed the streets and countrysides. Fifteen million men and women—one out of every four Americans—would soon be out of work.

The Depression hit baseball too. Attendance fell dramatically, because few people could afford to buy food, let alone a

PRECEDING PAGES—
RIGHT: THE CHICAGO
AMERICAN
GIANTS, 1927.
LEFT: J.L. WILKINSON
AND
THE KANSAS CITY
MONARCHS IN
FRONT OF THEIR
TEAM BUS, NICK-
NAMED DR. YAK, IN
THE 1930s.

fifty-cent ticket to the ballpark. The Eastern League had disbanded in 1928, and despite the efforts of the Monarchs' J. L. Wilkinson, the National League failed in 1931. Most of the teams survived by barnstorming, but now the road trips were longer and the players were paid only a fraction of what they had made before—when they were paid at all.

Fortunately, there were people who had the desire—and the means—to revive the league. One of them was Gus Greenlee, a black gambler from Pittsburgh, Pennsylvania, who was known as Big Red. Greenlee ran Pittsburgh's "numbers" racket—an illegal game in which a bettor picked a three-digit number and bet as little as a nickel. The 100-to-1 payoff meant that a person could win five dollars on a nickel bet. Runners, or messengers, went around black neighborhoods every day collecting bets and delivering payoffs. It was a popular and profitable enterprise that made Greenlee a rich man.

Greenlee also owned a nightclub called the Crawford Grill. It featured famous black musicians like Count Basie, Lena Horne, and Duke Ellington.

When Greenlee bought a local semi-pro team called the Pittsburgh Colored Giants, he renamed them the Crawford Colored

THE PITTSBURGH
CRAWFORDS IN
1932

Giants. Eventually the name was shortened to the Crawfords.

Pittsburgh's other black team, the Homestead Grays, was owned by Cum Posey, the son of a wealthy banker and real-estate developer. Posey had built the Grays into an all-star team. They had not been part of either black league, but they had played—and beaten—most of the teams. In 1931 they won 136 games and lost ten.

Posey often traveled with the Grays, booking the ballparks and looking after his players' every need. He even made sure they got their favorite sandwiches after the game.

But Posey's rival, Gus Greenlee, was determined to build the best team in black baseball. His method was simple—he bought up the finest players on the Homestead Grays.

One of them was Oscar Charleston. Although Charleston was nearing the end of his career, Greenlee hired him to manage the team as well as play first base.

Another player, center fielder James "Cool Papa" Bell, was such a fast runner that he could make it from first to third on a bunt. In one game he hit three inside-the-park home runs. A teammate who often roomed with Bell on the road swore that Bell could flip off a light switch and be in bed before the room was dark.

COOL PAPA BELL, MASTER OF THE INSIDE-THE-PARK HOME RUN

THE HOMESTEAD GRAYS, 1931. CUM POSEY IS AT THE FAR LEFT, IN KNICKERS.

Third baseman William "Judy" Johnson, nicknamed Mr. Sunshine because he was cheerful and optimistic, always seemed to know what the other team was going to do. He could figure out the opposing manager's hand signals just by watching him for a few innings. Then, by whistling a coded message, he'd pass the signals on to his teammates.

Catcher Josh Gibson, who already had a reputation for hitting 500-foot home runs, caught Greenlee's eye in 1931 when he slammed seventy-five homers for the Homestead Grays. By the next season he was playing for the Crawfords. Legend has it that the only home run ever hit out of Yankee Stadium was a Gibson blast during a Negro league game.

Buck O'Neil of the Kansas City Monarchs, who spent six decades in baseball as a first baseman, manager, coach, and scout, played with or against nearly every important black athlete in the game. He never forgot Josh Gibson.

JUDY JOHNSON *(BELOW LEFT)* HAD A KNACK FOR READING THE OTHER TEAM'S SIGNALS.

BUCK O'NEIL *(BELOW RIGHT)* PLAYED WITH OR AGAINST NEARLY EVERY IMPORTANT BLACK ATHLETE IN THE GAME.

LEONARD

WEST
PHILA
STARS

34

TAYLOR

BROWN
PHILA
STAR

1937

BUCK LEONARD OF
THE HOMESTEAD
GRAYS EASES INTO
FIRST IN A 1937
GAME AGAINST THE
PHILADELPHIA STARS.

"He and Ruth had power alike," O'Neil recalled, "but Ruth struck out maybe 115 times a year. Josh Gibson struck out maybe fifty times a year. The best hitter I've ever seen. Would have been outstanding [in the majors]. Would have rewritten the record book as far as home runs are concerned."

The Crawfords quickly became the strongest team in black baseball. "We played everywhere. In every ballpark," one Crawford player recalled. "And we won. Won like we invented the game."

Greenlee spared no expense for his team. When his players were refused permission to use the locker rooms at the Pittsburgh Pirates' Forbes Field, Greenlee decided to build his own stadium.

Completed in 1932, Greenlee Field cost $60,000 and seated 7,500. It was the first stadium ever built for a black team. Greenlee also bought the Crawfords a luxurious new Mack bus to travel in. On some

trips, he would squeeze his 6' 2" frame into the driver's seat and chauffeur his club himself for a day or two.

As the Depression grew worse, owners struggled to keep their teams going. The only people with money in the black community were gamblers like Gus Greenlee. Before long, most of the black teams were owned by "numbers kings."

THE PITTSBURGH CRAWFORDS POSE BEFORE THEIR CUSTOM-BUILT TOUR BUS IN FRONT OF THE ENTRANCE TO GREENLEE FIELD.

"THEY WOULD HAVE BEEN STEEL TYCOONS, AUTO MOGULS, HAD THEY BEEN WHITE."

—NOVELIST RICHARD WRIGHT ON
THE BLACK NUMBERS KINGS OF THE 1930s

Tom Wilson had the Baltimore Elite Giants; Alex Pompez, the Cuban Stars; Ed Bolden, the Philadelphia Stars. In New York the Black Yankees were supposedly owned by dancer Bill "Bojangles" Robinson, but Ed "Soldier Boy" Semler had really purchased the team. And in Newark, the Eagles were owned by Abe Manley, the numbers king of Trenton, and managed by his wife, Effa.

In 1931 Greenlee signed one of the greatest pitchers of all time—Leroy "Satchel" Paige. Paige had earned his nickname at age seven when he worked as a porter in a Mobile, Alabama, train station, carrying passengers' suitcases, or satchels. The pay was ten cents a bag. To make more money, Paige carried several bags at one time on a pole across his shoulders. Someone said he looked like "a walking satchel tree." Soon everyone was calling him Satchel.

Paige's main weapon was a blazing fastball. He had many names for it—Long Tom and Little Tom, the bee ball (so fast it hummed as it flew), jump ball, trouble ball, midnight rider, and four-day creeper. No matter what he called it, it was impossible to hit.

"He was tall," Cool Papa Bell said, "between 6' 3" and 6' 4", but he only weighed about 180, so it seemed like he was all arms and legs. He could put that big fastball right at your knees all day long. It seemed to come right out of his foot."

Above all, Satchel Paige was a great showman and crowd pleaser. He liked to arrive late so that he could make a grand entrance—sometimes with a police escort. Then he would take his time walking to the mound.

"I like walking slow," Paige said. "Moving that way got them to laugh. Laughing is a pretty sound. But I never joked when I was pitching."

On barnstorming trips, Paige often promised to strike out the first nine men he faced in a game—and he usually did. Sometimes he would call his outfielders in and finish an inning with just the infielders. The

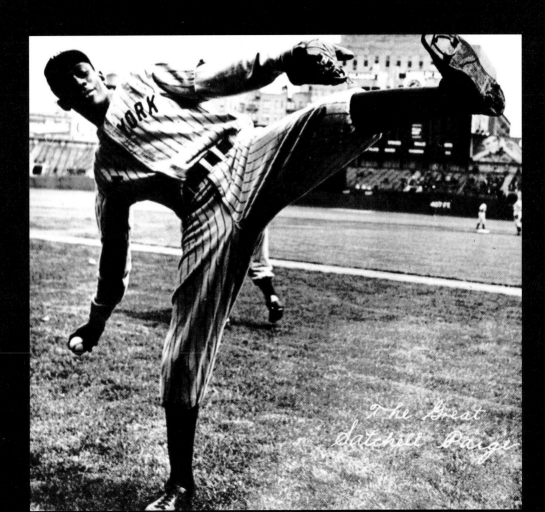

The Great
Satchell Paige

fans loved it. As Buck O'Neil said, Paige was "the guy that people wanted to see."

Like Ruth, Satchel had learned to play ball in reform school. When he was 12, he had stolen some toys from a store. A hard-hearted judge sent him to the Industrial School for Negro Children.

"My time there made me a man," Paige would always say. "I played ball, sang in the choir, and got a pretty fair education."

When he left reform school five years later, the Mobile Tigers gave him a tryout. After throwing ten unhittable strikes past the manager, Satchel signed his first contract—for one dollar a game.

Paige would sign many more contracts. If there was one thing he did better than pitching, it was jumping from team to team. He called himself "the travelin' man," and during his career he played for over 250 teams.

In January 1933 Greenlee put together a new Negro National League. There were six teams—the Crawfords, the Chicago American Giants, Columbus Blue Birds, Detroit Stars, Indianapolis ABCs (who were soon replaced by the Baltimore Black Sox), and Nashville Elite Giants.

When major league baseball had its first All-Star game in July 1933, in an attempt to bring fans into the ballpark and save their ailing businesses, Greenlee and the other black team owners thought that was a fine idea. Two months later they held the first all-black East-West All-Star game, in Chicago's Comiskey Park. Fans came from around the country to cheer on the teams they had helped pick with their votes in the Chicago *Defender* and the Pittsburgh *Courier,* two black weekly newspapers.

Unlike the black World Series, which never caught on because black fans didn't have the time or money to attend a series of games, the annual East-West All-Star game was an immediate success. The huge crowds sometimes numbered 50,000. It was "the glory part of our baseball," one player recalled.

THE CHICAGO
AMERICAN GIANTS,
1931

Buck O'Neil remembered how much the fans loved the game, and how far they would travel to see it:

"People would come, like we used to say, 'two to a mule.' We would have excursions running from New Orleans to Chicago. And they would pick people up in Mississippi, Memphis, Tennessee. Right

on to Chicago. And everybody came to that ball game. You would look up, and there's Joe Louis and Marva Louis [the black boxing champ and his wife] sitting in a box seat down front. All of the great entertainers in Chicago at that time. They would come and we had something to show. Yeah. We had something to show."

BUCK LEONARD STANDS FAR LEFT, IN A GRAYS UNIFORM. JOSH GIBSON, ALSO IN A GRAYS UNIFORM, STANDS THIRD FROM RIGHT.

CHAPTER 5

THE GREAT EXPERIMENT. Branch Rickey was an Ohio farm boy whose family's Methodist faith was at the center of their lives. He grew up pious and hardworking— and crazy about baseball, learning to play in the backyard with a ball sewn by his mother. To help pay his way through college, Rickey got a job coaching the baseball team, for whom he was also the catcher. Their star player was first baseman Charles "Tommy" Thomas, the only black man on the team. The racism that Thomas experienced made a lasting impression on Rickey.

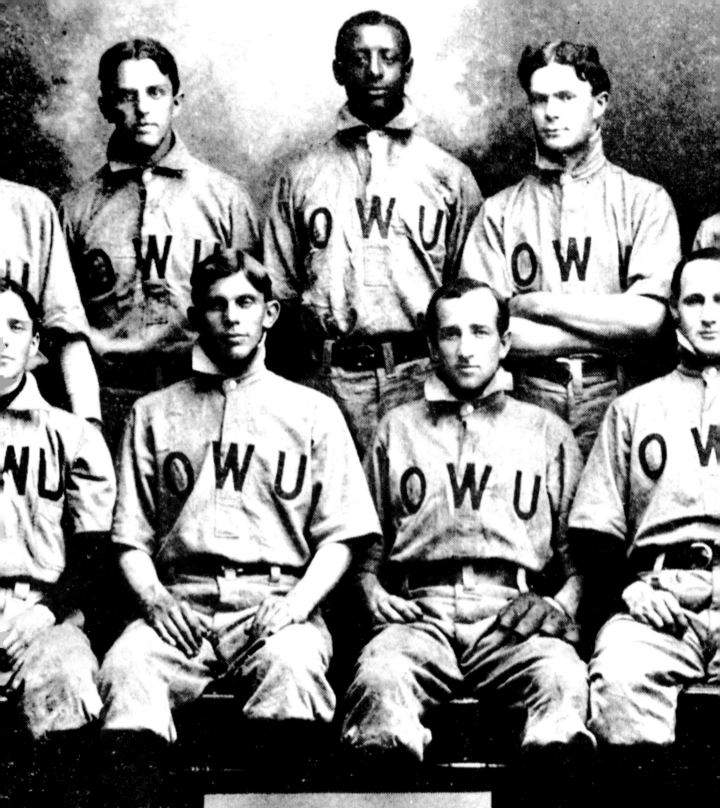

CHAMPIONS.
OF
OHIO.
1904.

BRANCH RICKEY,
BASEBALL'S GREAT
REVOLUTIONARY

On a road trip one season, a hotel refused Thomas a room. Rickey was outraged and finally persuaded the hotel manager to let Thomas room with him.

Later, when Rickey went to their room, he found a tense and brooding Thomas standing in the corner. Rickey tried to reassure him, but Thomas, angry and humiliated, was too upset.

"Tears spilled down his face," Rickey recalled years later, "and splashed on the floor. Then he rubbed one great hand over the other with all the power of his body, muttering 'Black skin...black skin. If I could only make 'em white.'"

After college Rickey played briefly with several professional teams, then became a lawyer. But he quickly returned to baseball as a scout, and by 1913 he was managing the St. Louis Browns.

In those days baseball players trained as little as possible. They would usually arrive at spring training overweight and out of shape. They believed they could "play themselves into shape" in a few short weeks—while still drinking and smoking after practice.

Branch Rickey had different ideas. He believed in a "scientific" method of baseball. In 1916 he crossed town to join the St. Louis Cardinals, where he made his players run wind sprints and practice sliding into sandpits. He would not allow them to drink, play poker, or swear during training. He started every day with a blackboard lecture on baseball tactics. His players didn't know what to make of him, but his efforts paid off, and the Cardinals began to win.

When Rickey saw how hard it was to acquire first-rate players from other teams, he developed a system of minor league clubs that he called "farm teams." These teams would "grow" new talent for the Cardinals. The idea worked brilliantly, and within a few years the farm teams were producing a steady supply of good young players ready to move up to the majors.

In 1943, after nearly thirty years with St. Louis, Rickey moved east and became president and general manager of the Brooklyn Dodgers. The Dodgers, who had never won a World Series, had most of the players they needed to win the pennant and maybe even the championship. Rickey intended to take them all the way—and he had a revolutionary plan for doing it.

Rickey believed the time was right to integrate baseball—to end segregation and sign black players to major league clubs. Black athletes were already competing against whites in other sports. Jesse Owens had won four gold medals in the 1936 Berlin Olympics. A year later Joe Louis won the world heavyweight boxing championship from Jim Braddock. World War II was raging overseas, and black and white soldiers were fighting and dying side by side.

JERRY BENJAMIN AT BAT FOR THE HOMESTEAD GRAYS, 1942

And there was money to be made. Black fans flocked to Negro league games, and the teams were flourishing. Rickey knew the same fans would come to major league games if black players were on the teams.

But integrating baseball would not be easy. Baseball commissioner Kenesaw Mountain Landis, who had been brought into baseball after the 1919 White Sox scandal to "clean up the game," was a lifelong opponent of integration. He had done everything he could to keep the old "gentleman's agreement" in effect. "The colored ballplayers have their own league," he said. "Let them stay in their own league."

In 1944 Landis died and was replaced by A. B. "Happy" Chandler, a former governor of Kentucky and a United States senator. Chandler proved to be a very different commissioner. When questioned about allowing blacks in major league baseball, he said, "I'm for the Four Freedoms. If a black boy can make it on Okinawa and Guadalcanal [two World War II battlefields], he can make it in baseball."

OPPOSITE: BLACK FANS PACK THE STANDS AT A HOMESTEAD GRAYS GAME. RICKEY KNEW THEY WOULD COME TO MAJOR LEAGUE GAMES IN EQUALLY BIG NUMBERS IF THEY COULD SEE BLACK PLAYERS.

BASEBALL COMMISSIONER KENESAW MOUNTAIN LANDIS, A LIFELONG OPPONENT OF INTEGRATION

"IF WE ARE ABLE TO STOP BULLETS, WHY NOT BALLS?"

—AFRICAN AMERICAN PICKET SIGN SEEN AT YANKEE STADIUM

Still, Rickey knew he would have to move carefully and choose just the right man to break the color barrier. He found that man in a talented young athlete named Jack Roosevelt Robinson.

Like Rickey, Jackie Robinson came from a poor family. He was born in Cairo, Georgia, in 1919, the grandson of a slave and one of five children of a sharecropper who deserted them when Jackie was a baby. Jackie's mother moved the family to Pasadena, California, where they were the only blacks in an all-white neighborhood. The white children threw rocks at the Robinson kids—until Jackie and his older brothers started throwing them back.

Robinson was a superb athlete and went to Pasadena Junior College and the University of California at Los Angeles (UCLA) on scholarships. He starred in football, basketball, track, and baseball. He was a strong, proud man who stood up for his rights.

During World War II, while Robinson was stationed in Texas, the army desegregated, ordering that whites and blacks must be treated equally on all its bases. But one day a bus driver told Robinson to sit in

AT UCLA, JACKIE ROBINSON WAS A STAR ATHLETE IN FOOTBALL, BASKETBALL, TRACK, AND BASEBALL.

the back of a military bus at Fort Hood. Robinson, who was one of the army's first black officers, refused even when he was told he would be arrested. He was given a court-martial—a military trial—and found not guilty. A few months later he received an honorable discharge and signed as a shortstop with the Kansas City Monarchs for $400 a month.

The Monarchs were one of the strongest teams in the Negro leagues. Owner J. L. Wilkinson had a good eye for talent and filled his roster with stars like Bullet Joe Rogan, Buck O'Neil, and Satchel Paige.

Wilkinson is also credited as the "father of night baseball." Although a few night games had been played as far back as 1880, the lights were never bright enough or very dependable. In 1930 Wilkinson designed a lighting system that was carried from field to field on the back of a truck. The lights were raised on fifty-foot telescoping poles and powered by a huge generator mounted on the Monarchs' touring bus. Attendance skyrocketed at night games, with the crowds some-times reaching 12,000.

"I WAS IN TWO WARS."

—JACKIE ROBINSON (*LEFT*), REFERRING TO
FIGHTING WORLD WAR II OVERSEAS
AND PREJUDICE AT HOME

In 1945, when Jackie Robinson signed with the Monarchs, he took an immediate dislike to playing in the Negro leagues. Baseball was not his favorite sport, and he hated the informality of the league—Satchel Paige seemed to come and go on his own private schedule, and in Baltimore one day the official scorekeeper left in the middle of the game. Robinson also hated the endless bus rides and the segregated hotels and restaurants.

Jackie was quiet and kept to himself. To some of his teammates, it seemed that he thought he was better than they were. But they were impressed by his determination to be treated with respect.

"We'd been going for thirty years to this filling station in Oklahoma where we would buy gas," Buck O'Neil recalled. "We had two fifty-gallon tanks on that [bus]. We'd buy the gas, but we couldn't use the rest room. Jackie wanted to use the rest room.

"The man said, 'Boy, you can't go to that rest room.'

"Jackie said, 'Take the hose out of the tank.' This guy ain't gonna sell one hundred gallons of gas in a whole month. 'If we can't go to the rest room, we won't get any gas here. We'll get it someplace else.'

"The man said, 'Well, you boys can go to the rest room, but don't stay too long.'

"So, actually, he started something there. Now, every place we would go we wanted to know first could we use the rest room. If we couldn't use the rest room—no gas."

Despite his unhappiness with barnstorming, Robinson had a great year with the Monarchs and finished the season with a .387 average.

Branch Rickey had heard about Robinson and thought he might be the man he was looking for. He sent one of his scouts to talk to Robinson.

Meanwhile, Rickey created a diversion to fool the other teams. He announced that the Dodgers were forming a black baseball club— the Brooklyn Brown Dodgers—as part of a new all-black league. Now Rickey could interview black players without arousing any suspicions.

COMING!   COMING!   COMING!
KANSAS CITY MONARCHS
NIGHT BASEBALL

We have successfully lighted every kind of a ball park in the country, including both Major Leagues, AND CAN REPEAT IN ALL OF THEM.

The Greatest Drawing Card Outside the Major Leagues

Headquarters 420 East Ninth St., Kansas City, Mo.

Actual Photograph of One of the Many Towers Supporting Our Flood Lights

Actual Photograph of Trucks Used to Transport the Monarch Lighting Plant and Towers

JACKIE ROBINSON
AND
BRANCH RICKEY

Rickey and Robinson met in Rickey's Brooklyn office on August 29, 1945. Rickey quickly got to the point. He knew that Robinson had the physical skill to play for the Dodgers. But, he said, the first black player would face more abuse from other players and fans than any athlete in the history of the game. Rickey spent the rest of the meeting demonstrating that abuse. He cursed and yelled, threatened and screamed, threw punches that barely missed Robinson's face.

Then he told Robinson, "You can't retaliate."

"Mr. Rickey, do you want a ballplayer who's afraid to fight back?" Robinson asked.

Rickey responded: "I want a ballplayer with guts enough *not* to fight back. You will symbolize a crucial cause. One incident, just one incident, can set it back twenty years."

Rickey asked Robinson to promise that he wouldn't retaliate, no matter what happened, for three years. After thinking it over, Jackie agreed. Rickey had found his man.

Two months later the Brooklyn Dodgers announced that they had signed Jackie Robinson and were sending him to play for the Montreal Royals, their International League farm club in Canada.

As Rickey had predicted, the other major league clubs did not support his move. They voted fifteen to one against letting Robinson into the league. But Happy Chandler overruled them and approved the deal.

From the very first game, Robinson was under tremendous pressure. He knew there were people who wanted to see him strike out every time and drop every ball so that he would fail and be sent back to the Negro leagues.

He ignored the taunts that Branch Rickey had warned him about. He did not complain when he had to stay in different, and inferior, hotels from his white teammates, or eat in "Negro" restaurants. But his silence took its toll. By the end of the season, Robinson was racked by stomach pain. His wife, Rachel, thought he might have a nervous breakdown.

Robinson held on, however, and had a great season. With Jackie leading the way, now playing second base, the Royals won the league championship and then the minor league Little World Series.

Even after such an outstanding year, Robinson would still have to prove himself when he moved up to Brooklyn. Some of the Dodgers were Southerners who didn't like the idea of playing with a black man. Three of them drew up a petition saying they didn't want Jackie on the team. When they presented the petition to Dodger manager Leo Durocher, he tore it up.

SINGER LENA HORNE VISITS THE MONTREAL ROYALS, WITH WHOM JACKIE ROBINSON PLAYED BEFORE MOVING UP TO THE DODGERS.

Spring training came and went without incident. The Dodgers moved Jackie to first base because they had veteran player Eddie Stanky at second.

Finally, on Opening Day, April 15, 1947, Jackie Robinson made history by becoming the first black man in modern times to play major league baseball. More than half of the 26,623 fans at Brooklyn's Ebbets Field that day were black. Robinson failed to get a hit in the game, but the crowd was thrilled. The Dodgers won, 5–3.

It was a tough season for Robinson. When Philadelphia arrived for a three-game series, he nearly cracked. Led by their manager, Ben Chapman, the Phillies pulled out all the stops. "Nigger," they yelled, "go back to the cotton fields!" "We don't want you here, nigger!" "Hey, snowflake!"

Only his promise to Branch Rickey kept Robinson from exploding. By the third game of the series, the rest of the Dodgers were fed up. Stanky, one of the players who had circulated the petition to keep

Robinson off the team, challenged the Philadelphia bench: "Listen!" he shouted. "Why don't you yell at somebody who can answer back?"

Later that season, when the Dodgers played Cincinnati and some fans started in on Robinson, Pee Wee Reese put his arm around his teammate's shoulder. Reese was a Southerner and a big favorite with the Cincinnati fans. His gesture quieted them immediately. Robinson was becoming a member of the team.

By the end of the season, Jackie Robinson had a .297 average, including twenty-nine stolen bases and twelve home runs. He was named Rookie of the Year by *The Sporting News*.

Robinson's aggressive, Negro league style of play had an immediate impact on the game.

"At the time [major league] baseball was a base-to-base thing," said Buck O'Neil. "You hit the ball, you wait on first base until somebody hit it again. But in our baseball you got on base if you walked, you stole second, you'd try to steal, they'd bunt you over to third and you actually score runs without a hit. This was our baseball."

Robinson and the other black players who followed him into the majors eventually made it everyone's baseball. Branch Rickey's "great experiment," as sportswriters came to call it, would succeed far better than anyone had imagined.

OPPOSITE: JACKIE ROBINSON STEALS HOME AGAINST YANKEE CATCHER YOGI BERRA IN THE 1955 WORLD SERIES.

BROOKLYN'S EBBETS FIELD, WHERE ROBINSON MADE HISTORY ON APRIL 15, 1947

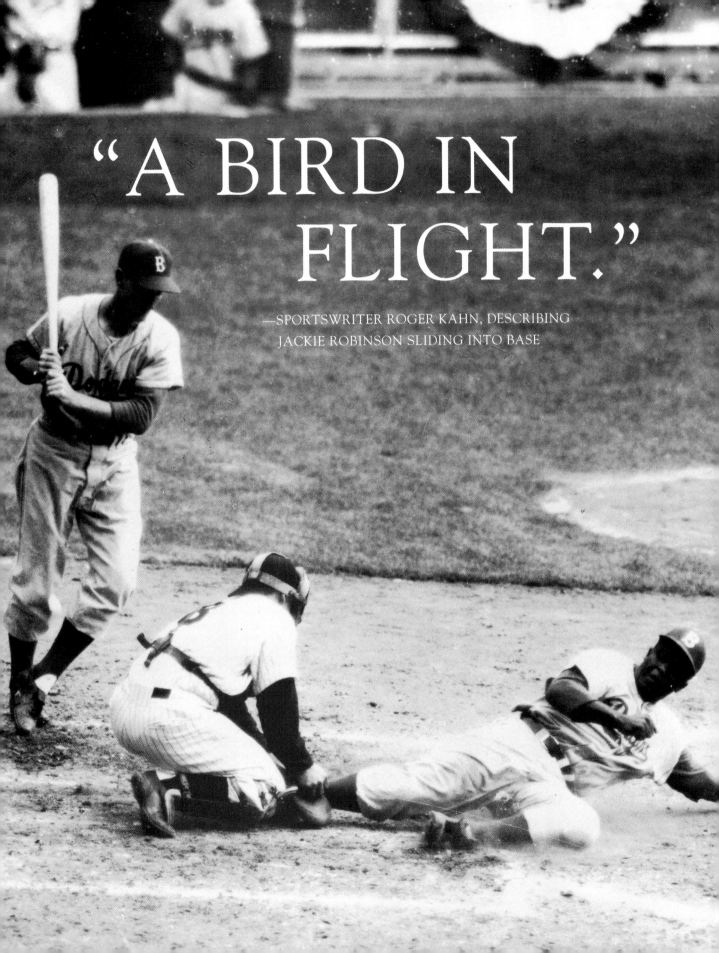

"A BIRD IN FLIGHT."

—SPORTSWRITER ROGER KAHN, DESCRIBING
JACKIE ROBINSON SLIDING INTO BASE

THE OLDEST ROOKIE IN THE GAME.

On July 9, 1948, a tall, not-so-young rookie walked slowly from the Cleveland Indians' bullpen to the pitching mound. "I didn't go fast," he remembered. "No reason wearing myself out just walking." That day Satchel Paige, who was either 38, 42, 44, or 48 years old (Satch liked to make himself younger or older depending on how well he was pitching), became the oldest rookie ever to play in organized baseball.

Paige had wanted to be the first black player in the majors. This was his chance to

PRECEDING PAGES:
SATCHEL PAIGE

BILL VEECK, OWNER OF THE
CLEVELAND INDIANS

prove how wrong the white world had been all these years. A lot of people thought that signing Satchel was just another publicity stunt by Bill Veeck, the flashy young owner of the Indians. The editor of *The Sporting News* wrote, "Were Satchel white, he would not have drawn a second thought from Veeck."

"If Satch were white," Veeck responded, "he would have been in the majors twenty-five years earlier and the question would not be before the house."

The Indians were behind 4–1 when Paige took the mound. After twenty-two years, his fastball wasn't the mighty weapon it had once been. The first batter he faced rapped a base hit to left field. Paige's teammates looked at one another—what was going on? Had Satchel lost his stuff?

Paige quickly put their fears to rest. He pitched two brilliant innings, dazzling the St. Louis Browns with the same pitches that had won him nearly 2,000 games in his Negro league career.

"I used my single windup," he said, "my triple windup, my hesitation windup, and my now windup…my step-and-pitch-it, my sidearm throw, and my bat dodger."

"I USED TO OVERPOWER 'EM; NOW I OUTCUTE 'EM."

—SATCHEL PAIGE

When he was the starting pitcher in a game against the Washington Senators, 72,000 fans jammed Cleveland Stadium, setting a new night-attendance record. Paige notched his first major league win, 4–3.

Paige finished the season with a 6–1 record. The Indians clinched the pennant and went on to win the World Series.

It turned out to be the high point of Paige's major league career, for age had indeed caught up with him and he never pitched as well again. He stayed with Cleveland for a while and then moved over to the St. Louis Browns. In 1954 he went back to barnstorming. One of his few regrets, he told a sportswriter, was that he'd never had a chance to strike out Babe Ruth in the major leagues.

In 1946 Branch Rickey had recruited another talented black player—catcher Roy Campanella, who had already spent nine years in the Negro leagues playing for the Baltimore Elite Giants.

Campanella, who was 25 when he joined the Dodgers, had grown up in an integrated neighborhood in Philadelphia. Until he was recruited by Baltimore at age 15, he did not know that blacks couldn't play in the majors.

When Campanella first met Branch Rickey, he assumed that Rickey wanted him to play for the Brown Dodgers. Like everyone else, Campanella had been fooled by Rickey's story about starting an all-black team. But Rickey wanted Campanella to be the first black catcher in the majors.

Campanella spent a year at the Dodgers' Nashua, New Hampshire, farm team and much of the following year with Montreal. In 1949 he took over behind home plate for the Dodgers.

ROY CAMPANELLA SPENT NINE YEARS IN THE NEGRO LEAGUES BEFORE SIGNING WITH THE DODGERS IN 1946.

ROY CAMPANELLA

"Mr. Rickey told me, 'You are going to have to be a diplomat to talk to the ten or eleven different pitchers on this team, to make them use your judgment in calling and giving all the signals. The catcher runs the team in the major leagues.'"

Campanella ran the Dodgers for nearly ten years and was named the National League Most Valuable Player three times.

Just as Campanella moved up to the major leagues, Jackie Robinson's three years of silence ended. He had turned the other cheek just as he'd promised Branch Rickey. Now things would be different. "They better be prepared to be rough this year," he said, "because I'm going to be rough on them."

Robinson became more aggressive on the field and more assertive when away from it. In St. Louis he demanded—and got—a room in the same hotel as the rest of the team. He encouraged black fans to demand "what you got coming." Some sportswriters who had once applauded him began to criticize him, saying he should be a player and not a crusader.

Robinson fired back: "As long as I appeared to ignore insult and injury, I was a martyred hero to a lot of people. But the minute I began to sound off—I became a swell-headed wise-guy, an 'uppity nigger.'"

But Robinson's anger didn't affect his playing. He had his best season ever, leading the league in batting average and stolen bases and finishing second in RBIs. So many fans came out to see him play when the Dodgers were on the road that the team accounted for one third of the entire National League's attendance. When the season ended, Robinson was voted Most Valuable Player.

AS HIS WIFE, RACHEL,
WATCHES NERVOUSLY,
JACKIE ROBINSON
CRASHES HIS WAY INTO
HOME PLATE.

In 1951 Leo Durocher, who was now manager of the New York
Giants, needed a center fielder for his club. He heard about an
outfielder playing for the Birmingham Black Barons named Willie
Mays. Mays had everything—speed, a great glove, and a powerful bat.
The Giants purchased Mays's contract from the Barons and sent him
to their farm club. He hit a hot .357 in Trenton, New Jersey, and then
an unbelievable .477 in Minneapolis, Minnesota.

Mays, the oldest of twelve children, was born in Westfield,
Alabama, in 1931. His father had been a star in a local industrial
league. He had started Willie playing baseball before he could walk,
rolling a ball to him across the living room floor. By the time Mays
was 16 he was playing for the Barons, but home games only—his
teachers said no to road games because they were afraid Willie
wouldn't do his homework.

"WHEN I WAS 17, I REALIZED I WAS IN A FORM OF SHOW BUSINESS."

—WILLIE MAYS

When Durocher told Mays, who was only 19, that he wanted to bring him up to the Giants in 1951, Mays panicked. He didn't think he was ready for the majors. Durocher tried to reassure him—he didn't have to hit .477 for the Giants; .250 would be fine. Mays agreed to give it a try.

At first his fears seemed justified. He went 1 for 26 at the plate. One day Durocher found him crying in the dugout after a game.

"Mr. Leo," said Mays, "I just can't hit up here."

"As long as I'm manager of the Giants," Durocher answered, "you're my center fielder."

Mays got two hits the next day and snapped out of his slump. His hard hitting and astonishing fielding skills electrified the Giants, and they went on to win the pennant in 1951. When it was over, Durocher said, "If he could cook, I'd marry him."

Willie was outgoing but not good at remembering names. Whenever he saw a familiar face, he would greet the person with "Say hey." Soon he was called the Say Hey Kid. He was a great showman, too. He always wore a cap that was too large so that it would fly off his head as he chased long fly balls in center field.

Willie Mays spent twenty-two years in the majors and had one of the most outstanding careers in professional baseball history. He led the league in home runs four times, hitting fifty-two in 1965, and finished his career with 660.

Another home run hitter came into the majors from the Negro leagues at the same time as Mays. Hank Aaron had started playing ball with the semi-pro Black Bears in his hometown of Mobile, Alabama, while he was still in high school. His next stop was with the Indianapolis Clowns, where he hit .467 and led the Negro American League as a rookie.

Like many young blacks at the time, Aaron had been inspired by Jackie Robinson's success in the majors.

"I felt that if Jackie could play in the big leagues and make it, Henry Aaron could do the same thing," he said. "I knew it was going to be a hard road, but I felt like if Jackie could do it, then he had given every black kid in America that little ray of hope that they could do it."

Aaron signed with the Milwaukee Braves in 1952 and was sent to their Jacksonville farm club in the South Atlantic, or Sally, League. He did well in Jacksonville and was named Most Valuable Player for the 1953 season, but he hated the racism he encountered in the all-Southern league.

HANK AARON

"I was one of the first blacks playing in the Sally League," Aaron remembered. "I was literally going through hell down there. Name-calling, racial slurs, resentment for playing against whites."

Jacksonville's manager, Ben Geraghty, visited Aaron in his room nearly every night to talk to him and help keep him going.

Aaron moved up to the Braves in 1954 as their center fielder, and by 1956 he had won his first batting championship with a league-leading .328 average. The next season he led the Braves in their conquest of the Yankees in the World Series.

The Braves moved to Atlanta in 1966, and season after season Aaron added to his home run total. He hit so many that fans began to call him the Hammer. Nearly twenty years after joining the majors, he passed the 700 mark.

Suddenly fans and sportswriters woke up to an incredible possibility: Babe Ruth's record of 714 career homers just might be broken.

A lot of people didn't want to see Ruth's record overtaken—especially by a black man—and Aaron began to receive hate mail. Many of the letters threatened to harm Aaron or kidnap his children if he didn't stop.

Hank kept silent about the hate mail, but word soon got out and letters of support began to flood in. "I don't care what color you are," a 12-year-old wrote. "What do these fans want you to do? Just quit hitting?"

Aaron began the 1974 season two homers short of breaking Ruth's record. The pressure was tremendous. Over 300 reporters were traveling with the Braves, waiting for history to be made.

On April 5, 1974, Aaron tied Ruth's record. Three days later, with his proud parents sitting in the stands, he hit a pitch over the left field fence to break Babe Ruth's record.

He remembered how he felt as he rounded the bases:

"I was in my own little world. It was like running in a bubble, and I could see all these people jumping up and down and waving their arms in slow motion. Every base seemed crowded, like there were all these people I had to get through to make it to home plate.

I just couldn't wait to get there. I was told I had a big smile on my face as I came around third. I purposely never smiled as I ran the bases after a home run, but I suppose I couldn't help it that time."

The game was halted for a ceremony at home plate. Hank hugged his parents and family. How did he feel? a reporter asked.

"Thank God it's over," Aaron said.

By the end of his career, Hank Aaron had hit 755 home runs—a record that still stands today.

"THE ONLY MAN I IDOLIZE MORE THAN MYSELF."

—MUHAMMAD ALI, FORMER BOXING CHAMPION,
SPEAKING ABOUT HANK AARON

CHAPTER 7

THE DEATH KNELL FOR OUR
BASEBALL. Team by team, black athletes
followed Jackie Robinson into the majors.
Don Newcombe joined the Dodgers right
after Roy Campanella, in 1946. The
Newark Eagles' Larry Doby, who led the
Negro leagues with a .414 average, was
signed by the Cleveland Indians in 1947.
That same year, Hank Thompson and
Willard Brown of the Kansas City
Monarchs joined the St. Louis Browns.
Most of the big league clubs didn't pay
the Negro league teams by buying

LARRY DOBY, WHO
FOLLOWED JACKIE
ROBINSON INTO
THE MAJORS

OPPOSITE: THE
NEWARK EAGLES,
1946

up the players' contracts, as they did when they hired a player away from a major or minor league team. Even Branch Rickey, who signed up sixteen players for the Brooklyn organization, had an excuse for this theft of talent.

Many of the Negro league owners were numbers runners, Rickey told reporters. That made the league a "racket" that wasn't entitled to compensation.

Effa Manley, manager of the Newark Eagles, fired back. "He took players from the Negro leagues and didn't even pay for them. I'd call that a racket."

But no one wanted to slow down the integration of the major leagues. "It was the death knell for our baseball," said Buck O'Neil. "But who cared? Who cared?"

The Negro leagues struggled on for a few more years. But as the better players left for the majors, the teams became mere shadows of themselves. Black fans began following major league teams with black players.

Jackie Robinson's Brooklyn Dodgers were wildly popular. When they played in Cincinnati, Ohio, black fans took a train nicknamed the Jackie Robinson Special, which ran from Norfolk, Virginia—600 miles away— so they could see their hero play.

Most Negro leaguers would never be asked to join the majors. They were too old or not good enough to take a white regular's spot. At the same time their jobs were in danger because attendance at Negro league games was plunging and the leagues were collapsing. Every team was losing money.

At the end of the 1949 season the New York Black Yankees and the Newark Eagles closed their doors forever. It was the end of the Negro National League.

Some of the other teams survived for a few years by barnstorming, but by 1953 there were fewer blacks playing ball for a living—in any league—than at any time in the century. The Negro American League, now composed of only four teams, survived until 1960.

In 1957, Walter O'Malley, who now owned the Brooklyn Dodgers, announced that he was moving the team to Los Angeles, California. Roy Campanella, the Dodgers' star catcher, did not accompany the team. In January 1958 he was permanently paralyzed when his car skidded on ice and crashed into a telephone pole.

Jackie Robinson chose to retire rather than move west. He had been a symbol of integration for thousands of African Americans. Now he became more active in his crusade for racial equality, refusing to attend old-timers' games because there were no blacks in baseball management.

In 1962 Robinson was elected to the Baseball Hall of Fame—the first African American to receive that honor.

Three years later, the United States Congress passed the Civil Rights Act of 1965. The act forbade segregation in public places. Black players could now stay in the same hotels and eat in the same restaurants as their white teammates in every state in the union.

That same year Branch Rickey died. Jackie Robinson attended the funeral with several ex-teammates, including Bobby Bragan, who had tried to keep Robinson off the team. Now Bragan came to honor Rickey because, as he said, Rickey had made him a better man.

The following June, Ted Williams was inducted into the Hall of Fame. Like many white players of his era, Williams had faced some of the great Negro league stars in exhibition games. Now, in his acceptance speech, the Red Sox slugger talked about the exclusion of Negro league players from the Hall of Fame:

"I hope someday Satchel Paige and Josh Gibson can be added here as a symbol of the great Negro league players. They are not here only because they didn't get a chance."

AT HIS HALL OF FAME INDUCTION IN 1966, TED WILLIAMS *(ABOVE)* CALLED FOR THE INCLUSION OF NEGRO LEAGUE PLAYERS IN THE HALL.

OPPOSITE: JACKIE ROBINSON LEAVES THE DODGERS' DRESSING ROOM FOR THE LAST TIME.

SATCHEL PAIGE
BEFORE HIS HALL
OF FAME PLAQUE

Five years later, in 1971, Paige became the first Negro league player to enter the Hall of Fame. He was followed in 1972 by Josh Gibson and Buck Leonard, the Homestead Grays' first baseman. Eventually seven other Negro leaguers were selected by a special committee: Rube Foster, Cool Papa Bell, Judy Johnson, Newark Eagles' third baseman Ray Dandridge, Pop Lloyd, Oscar Charleston, and Cuban pitcher Martin Dihigo. Today there is a section of the Hall of Fame devoted to the Negro leagues and the history of black baseball.

SOME OF THE NEGRO LEAGUE STARS WHO MADE IT INTO THE HALL OF FAME: CLOCKWISE FROM TOP LEFT: BUCK LEONARD (INDUCTED 1972);
COOL PAPA BELL (1974) WITH HIS WIFE, CLARABELLE; JUDY JOHNSON (1975), AND JOHN L. USRY, ACCEPTING FOR POP LLOYD IN 1977
(LLOYD DIED IN 1965), BOTH WITH COMMISSIONER BOWIE KUHN.

"JACKIE STOLE HOME AND HE'S SAFE."

—REVEREND JESSE JACKSON AT JACKIE ROBINSON'S FUNERAL

JUST 10 DAYS BEFORE HIS DEATH, JACKIE ROBINSON THROWS OUT THE FIRST BALL AT THE FIRST GAME OF THE 1972 WORLD SERIES. BOWIE KUHN STANDS AT HIS SIDE.

Jackie Robinson's last public appearance was at the opening game of the 1972 World Series in Cincinnati. He was 53 years old and suffering from diabetes and heart disease, but he was still crusading for more opportunities for blacks in baseball. Before he threw out the first ball, Robinson had this to say:

"I am extremely proud and pleased to be here this afternoon but must admit, I'm going to be tremendously more pleased and more proud when I look at that third base coaching line one day and see a black face managing baseball."

Jackie Robinson died less than two weeks later.

Since that time, few blacks have had the opportunity to manage a big league team. And even though the winning manager of the 1992 and 1993 World Series was a black man—Cito Gaston of the Toronto Blue Jays—the first four decades of integrated play have produced only a handful of black managers. Bill White, the black broadcaster and former first baseman, was president of the National League from 1989 to 1993. But there are still no black owners.

Baseball is not perfect—it reflects both the strengths and weaknesses of American society. When Jackie Robinson stepped onto Ebbets Field from the shadows of the Negro leagues, many hoped it would bring an end to racism in America. It was a good beginning, but it also marked a loss for African Americans.

The Negro leagues were a source of pride for black people throughout the country. They had employed hundreds of blacks and poured thousands of dollars back into the black community. They had enabled some of the finest athletes in America to earn a living playing a game they loved.

"Because of baseball," said Cool Papa Bell, "I smelled the rose of life. I wanted to meet interesting people, to travel and to have nice clothes. Baseball allowed me to do all those things, and most important, it allowed me to become a member of a brotherhood of friendship which will last forever."

The Negro leagues withered away during the 1950s, finally dissolving completely in 1964. The last original Negro league team, the Indianapolis Clowns, played their final game in 1968.

Negro league records are sketchy because reporters did not write many stories about black athletes until Jackie Robinson broke into the majors in 1947.

Recently, however, people have been filling the gaps in those records—donating photographs to libraries and combing through box scores in old newspapers—in order to create an accurate picture of the leagues. Their efforts will guarantee that the accomplishments of these remarkable athletes—and their place in American history—survive beyond the memory of the players who still live and the people who were lucky enough to see them play.

"THERE WAS ALWAYS SUN SHINING SOMEPLACE."

—JUDY JOHNSON, RECALLING LIFE ON THE ROAD IN THE NEGRO LEAGUES

INDEX

Page numbers in **boldface** refer to illustrations.